Searchlight
BOOKS™

How Do
We Use
Money?

Budgeting, Spending, and Saving

Bitsy Kemper

Lerner Publications
Minneapolis

Lerner Publications Company
A division of Lerner Publishing Group, Inc.
241 First Avenue North
Minneapolis, MN 55401 USA

For reading levels and more information, look up this title at
www.lernerbooks.com.

Content consultant: Donna Little, Associate Professor of Accounting and
Finance, Menlo College

Library of Congress Cataloging-in-Publication Data

Kemper, Bitsy.
    Budgeting, spending and saving / by Bitsy Kemper.
        pages   cm. — (Searchlight books : how do we use money?)
    Includes index.
    ISBN 978-1-4677-5228-2 (lib. bdg. : alk. paper)
    ISBN 978-1-4677-6252-6 (eBook)
    1. Money—Juvenile literature. 2. Savings accounts—Juvenile literature.
3. Budgets, Personal—Juvenile literature. 4. Finance, Personal—Juvenile
literature. I. Title.
HG221.5.K46 2015
332.024—dc23   2014017712

Manufactured in the United States of America
1 – BP – 12/31/14

Contents

Chapter 1

SPENDING MONEY

Money makes our world work. Adults earn money by doing jobs. Kids may receive allowances. Everyone buys products and services. The people who make products or perform services get paid. Money moves from person to person. It can seem like money comes and goes too quickly.

Kids often get spending money from their parents. How do adults earn money?

Money is much easier to spend than to earn. Many people develop bad money habits.

The good news is that smart money habits are easy to learn. Kids who learn them become adults who make good money choices. Poor money choices may mean you cannot see a movie with friends. Adults face more serious problems with money. They might not have enough money to pay bills. Learning good money habits can prevent these problems.

Unpaid bills can start to pile up if adults have bad spending habits.

Skateboards are an example of something you might want but do not need.

Wants and Needs

Money is used to pay for two kinds of things. First, money can buy goods. This includes things such as an apple or a bicycle. Second, money can pay for services. Concerts and skiing lessons are examples of services. What kinds of goods and services do you spend money on?

The study of money is called economics. Two basic ideas in economics are *wants* and *needs*. A *need* is something you must have to survive. Needs include food, shelter, and clothing. A *want* is something you would like to have. But you can survive without it. Wants include fancy houses and skateboards.

You cannot buy everything you want. People must make decisions about what goods and services to purchase. Wants should be purchased after all your needs are met. Purchasing decisions can be difficult. They are affected by prices, what friends and parents think, and the ads or commercials we see.

Shop Smart!

Being an informed consumer is important. Companies spend billions of dollars trying to sell products. But you cannot always trust what companies say. They could be leaving out negative things about their products. It is useful to find out what real people think. You can ask friends if they have used a product. You can also read reviews online.

Reading reviews online can show you how similar products stack up against one another.

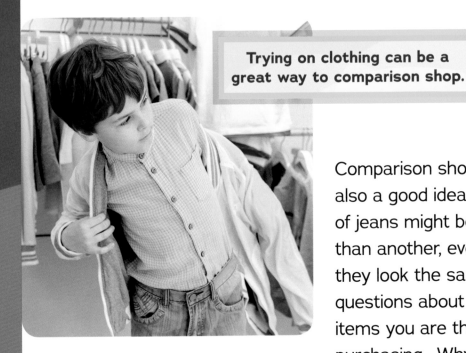

Trying on clothing can be a great way to comparison shop.

Comparison shopping is also a good idea. One pair of jeans might be cheaper than another, even though they look the same. Ask questions about the items you are thinking of purchasing. Why is one product more expensive? Is the extra cost worth it?

There are many ways to spend less money. Paying attention to brands can be helpful. Some brands of products cost more than others. Sometimes this is a sign of higher quality. Other times, it just means the brand is popular. People may be willing to pay more for it. Also, a company might spend a lot of money on advertising. Then they charge more for their products. You may be able to find a cheaper item that works just as well. You could buy a used item rather than a new one. Buying last year's version is another way to save.

Decision Time

You cannot wait to get a tablet computer that you can use to read books. However, you know it is important to be an informed consumer. You have looked online to find out more about two models. This chart has your notes about both. Which model would you choose? What features are most important to you?

Features	Model 1	Model 2
Release date	Already out	Two months from now
Price	$129	$199
Battery life	24 hours	12 hours
Screen size	6 inches (15 cm)	6 inches
Weight	Heavy	Light
Number of books	100	100

But shoppers should be careful when making these decisions. Will buying last year's model cost you more in the long run? Could it break or wear out sooner? What do online reviews tell you? Informed consumers find the answers to these questions. Of course, the simplest way to save money is to buy fewer things.

Opportunity Costs

When buying goods, it is important to think about what else you could have purchased. What are you giving up by choosing one thing instead of another? This is known as the opportunity cost. If you do not buy jeans for $90, what else can you do with that money? Thinking about this can help you make better decisions.

Some people save money by simply owning fewer things than others.

SEEING OPPORTUNITY COSTS

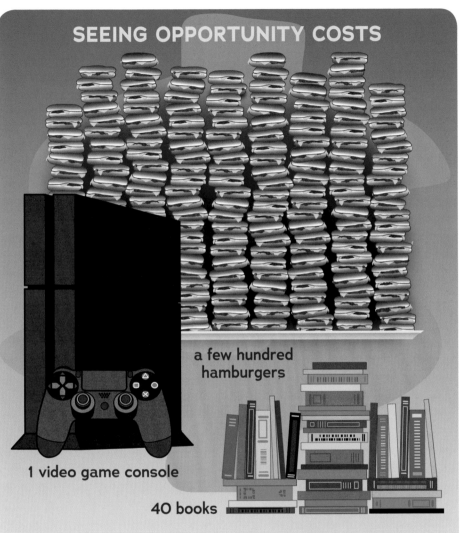

a few hundred hamburgers

1 video game console

40 books

Each stack of items has approximately the same value. You can think of one stack as the opportunity cost of another stack. Instead of buying a video game console for $400, you could purchase a few hundred hamburgers. Or you could buy the game console instead of forty books. If you had the chance to buy one stack, which would you choose? Which gives you the best value?

Chapter 2

SETTING GOALS

Making goals requires planning. If your goal were to play in the soccer championships, you would have a plan. Practice and hard work go into these kinds of goals. Planning makes reaching these goals possible. Financial goals are similar. They need planning too.

Taking home a soccer trophy is the result of hard work. What do this kind of goal and financial goals have in common?

Your goal might be a dollar amount. Maybe you want to save for a $60 video game. Or you might have a time-based goal. You will save as much as you can during the summer.

PLAYING A COOL NEW VIDEO GAME MAY BE THE REWARD FOR MEETING YOUR SAVINGS GOAL.

▼

Short- and Long-Term Goals

Short-term goals are for goods or services that cost little money. You can save up for these goals in a short amount of time. A parent might save to eat at a fancy restaurant. Kids might save to take a friend out for ice cream.

Long-term goals may take months or years to reach. For a grown-up, this might include saving to buy a car or a house. Kids make less money than grown-ups, so their goals are different. You might save long term to buy a bicycle. One very long-term goal is saving money for college. No matter the goal, saving money should be a habit that lasts a lifetime.

Treating a friend to ice cream is an example of a short-term savings goal.

Decision Time

You want to buy your grandma a gift for her birthday. She will be turning sixty-five in six weeks. You would love to give her both a $40 coat and a $20 calendar. You saw a great coat at a mall. You also found a cool calendar online. But you might end up buying only one or the other. It depends on how much money you can save. You earn a $10 allowance each week. You write out a few goals that you could choose from.

Goal option 1: You put away all $10 of your allowance each week. By the sixth week, you have $60 saved. However, you will not be able to buy anything for yourself during those six weeks.
Goal option 2: You put away $8 of your allowance each week. By the sixth week, you have $48 saved. You also get to keep $2 of your allowance each week.

Which option would you choose? Would one be more difficult for you than the other? Which presents would you be able to buy after reaching the goals? Don't forget to estimate taxes and shipping costs!

Steps

Breaking down the steps needed to reach a goal can make it easier to reach. The first step is to figure out exactly what your goal is. A new cell phone may cost $99. But this is not the total cost. Tax will be added if you buy the phone at a store. Buying it online may add shipping costs. You can plan ahead and add these costs to your savings goal. There is a chance the price could go up in the future.

$18.00

In the United States, tax is usually not included on price tags. In most other countries, the number on the price tag does include sales tax.

You may want to add a little extra money to your goal in case this happens. The second step is to figure out how much money you can set aside in a given period. How much can you save each week? You can then calculate how long it should take to reach your goal.

Calculating taxes, spending, and savings takes some work, but it pays off when you reach your goals.

Expect the Unexpected

Taxes and shipping costs can often be figured out ahead of time. But savers should plan for unexpected things too. What happens to a family's savings goal when a car breaks down and needs an expensive repair? What if you are two weeks away from buying a guitar and you accidentally break a neighbor's window? It is always a good idea to have an emergency fund. Having money set aside lets you keep your savings goals on track.

An accidentally broken window is an example of an emergency expense kids could face.

Did You Know?

More than half of American adults do not have large emergency funds. A 2011 survey asked people if they could afford a sudden $1,000 expense. This could be a car repair or a medical bill. About 64 percent of them said they would not be able to afford it. Large emergency funds are important for adults to have. But kids should set aside money too. What if you accidentally break your mom's vase? Or lose the video game a friend lent to you? Emergency funds can help you cover these unexpected expenses.

Chapter 3

SAVING

People often put time or effort into things that will pay off later. You might wait an hour to ride a roller coaster you enjoy. Athletes train for years before playing a professional sport. Financial goals take time too.

Waiting in line for a roller coaster is a lot less fun than riding one. But people still wait in line. Why? How is this similar to reaching your financial goals?

But saving your money is time well spent. Setting up an emergency fund can be a part of your goal.

Imagine you earn $8 per week. Your goal is to save $40 for a new telescope. You also want to save for an emergency fund. Each week, you put aside $4 for the telescope. Another $2 goes into the emergency fund. You get $2 to spend on other items each week.

Setting aside money in a special container is a great way to save for small purchases.

Setting aside money for an emergency fund means it takes you a little longer to save for the telescope, but not by much. You would save up the $40 in two and a half months. By that time, you would also have $20 put away for emergencies. Many people save in several accounts at once. One account might be for a vacation. Another could be for a car. And a third might be for college.

IT IS EASY TO TRACK SEVERAL ACCOUNTS USING ONLINE BANKING APPS FOR SMARTPHONES.

▼

3G

9:30 AM

MOBILE BANKING

Available Balance
$12,395.25

My Checking
Available Balance

My Savings
Available Balance
$2,739.84

Some kids keep their money in piggy banks.

Ways to Save

You can save money in different ways. The simplest is to store it at home. You might keep it in a piggy bank. The benefit is that your money is available at any time. The downside is that the money could be lost or stolen.

You can also put money into an account at a bank or a credit union. These two places are similar. But they have a few key differences. Banks are businesses. They make money by charging interest. They also make money by investing. Credit unions are not businesses. They belong to the people that deposit money into them. These people are called members. Credit unions do not try to earn money. Instead, extra money goes back to their members.

One good thing about using a bank or a credit union is that your money

Banks store their money in secure rooms called vaults.

is safe. The Federal Deposit Insurance Corporation (FDIC) insures bank accounts. The FDIC is part of the US government. Even if the bank or the credit union burns down, the government will give you the money you lost. However, there are downsides to banks and credit unions. You usually need to visit them when you want to get your money. Unlike with a piggy bank, the money isn't available right away.

Decision Time

Imagine you wanted to save for a $25 book. The book comes out next month, so you have a chance to save up for it. Would you save your money in your piggy bank? Or would you deposit the money into a bank account instead? What if you were saving up for a $350 gaming console? Figure out the pros and cons of each option. Which saving method is best for which kind of savings goals?

You can visit a bank to find out how much interest the bank's accounts offer.

Interest

When you put money in a savings account, you are loaning it to the bank. In return, the bank pays you interest. This is a percentage of the money in the account. Money kept at home earns no interest.

Interest makes your money grow over time. The longer it stays in the account, the more you earn. If you had $100 and a bank paid 4 percent interest each year, they would give you $4 at the end of the year. This may not sound like much. But the more money you have, the more interest you earn. Plus, the interest builds on itself. The next time the bank pays interest, it would be 4 percent of $104, or $4.16. This is called compound interest. In other words, your interest begins earning its own interest. Over time, the money can really add up.

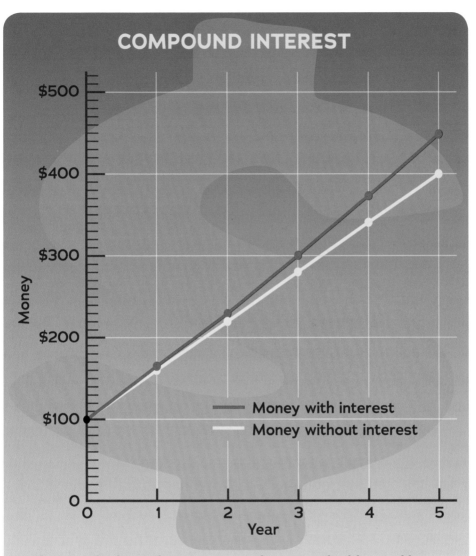

COMPOUND INTEREST

Money with interest
Money without interest

This graph shows how compound interest builds quickly. You start with $100 in your account. Each month, you add $5. The account earns 4 percent compound interest each year. By the second year, you have doubled your money. By the end of the fifth year, you have almost $450! Nearly $50 of that is interest alone.

It's important to look closely at your account's interest rates and extra fees.

Different banks and credit unions offer different interest rates. These rates change all the time. They can go up and down. The interest rate in most accounts is much less than 4 percent. Some banks and credit unions charge you extra fees. If you have too little money in your account, you may have to pay a fee. You have to keep enough money in the account to avoid these fees. Be sure to research several banks and credit unions to find the best deal.

Inflation

Inflation is a rise in the prices of goods and services. An item that was $10 a few years ago may now be $15.

Inflation decreases the value of money. That $100 in your bank account today cannot buy as much as it could last year. Imagine the $20 board game you want becomes $25 by the time you are ready to buy it. It is the exact same board game. Nothing new has been added. Only the price changed. The increase to $25 means your entire budget suffers. Your money is worth less than it used to be.

Did You Know?

You can see inflation in the prices of everyday products. One hundred years ago, a candy bar cost about 3¢. When your grandparents were kids in the 1940s or the 1950s, the price rose to 5¢. The price stayed the same until the late 1960s, when it jumped to 10¢. Your parents likely paid up to 40¢ for the same treat when they were kids. In 2014, candy bars cost up to $1 or more. What do you think a candy bar will cost your grandchildren?

Chapter 4

CREATING A BUDGET

The best way to be smart with money is to create a budget. Budgeting combines several good money habits. It helps you figure out wants and needs. It lets you make better purchasing decisions. It helps you reach

Your parents can assist you when you create your first budget. What does creating a budget help you do?

your financial goals. With a budget, you will have a plan to buy what is most important to you.

Money In

The first part of a budget is how much money you have coming in. You may not have a job yet, but you might earn an allowance. You may receive money on your birthday. You might even earn extra money for getting good grades or helping around your home. Adding up all this money tells you how much you can spend and save.

There are thousands of products to choose from in stores. Having a budget will help you make purchasing decisions about them.

Money Out

Where and how do you spend your money? Think about the last year. How many songs did you download? How many computer games or snacks did you buy? What about movie tickets, toys, or books? Did you donate money to charity? Try to think of every place your money goes. These are all parts of the "money out" side of a budget.

KIDS USUALLY SPEND CASH WHEN THEY MAKE PURCHASES. ADULTS OFTEN PAY IN OTHER WAYS, SUCH AS CREDIT CARDS OR DEBIT CARDS.

Did You Know?

The United States has a budget too. The president writes a plan for what the country should buy. Then Congress looks at the president's plan and makes changes. Finally, the budget is approved. The "money in" side includes income from taxes. The "money out" side includes spending on the military, roads, and schools.

Putting It All Together

Once you figure out how much is coming in and going out, you can make purchasing decisions. Adults must pay for needs first. This includes things such as food, house payments, and doctor bills. Kids usually do not have to pay for needs. Their parents cover their needs.

If you have a savings goal, you should start by putting money toward it. Then you can figure out which wants to purchase. Music, snacks, and books are some wants you might choose. Each time you spend money, record it in your budget.

After people know how much they can spend, they can begin deciding which products to buy.

SAMPLE BUDGETING SHEET

Budget for June

Income	Savings and Spending
Allowance: $30	Lemonade stand expenses: $25
Mowing lawns: $20	Gas for lawn mower: $10
Lemonade stand: $30	Money into savings: $10
Good grades: $20	New book: $15
	Amusement park ticket: $15
	Donation to animal charity: $5
Total: $100	Money into emergency fund: $20
	Total: $100

Here is a sample budgeting sheet. Take a look at the income column. Then read the savings and spending column. Imagine this is your budget. Would you add or take away anything? What could you do to spend less money? How could you boost your savings?

Looking at your budget can help improve your money habits. Were all the purchases you made worth it? Was there anything you could have borrowed instead of bought? Maybe you spent more than you remembered on fast food last month. It is easy to see these things when you keep track of spending. You can learn from past budgets. Budgeting is one of the most important good money habits.

SMART BUDGETING CAN BOOST YOUR SAVINGS AND GIVE YOU MORE MONEY TO SPEND ON THE THINGS YOU REALLY WANT.

Top Ten Things to Know

1. Wants are different from needs.

2. You cannot buy everything you want and need. You must make purchasing decisions.

3. You will save money if you are an informed consumer.

4. Thinking about opportunity costs will help you make better money decisions.

5. Giving up several little things now might help you buy something really big later on.

6. Putting money into a savings account is like paying yourself first.

7. Budgets help keep track of money coming in and money going out.

8. Whether you have long-term or short-term goals, it is never too early to start planning a budget.

9. Emergency funds help pay for unexpected expenses while keeping you within your budget.

10. Interest changes the amount of money, and inflation changes the value of money.

Glossary

bank: a business that holds and lends people's money

budget: a list of all sources of money coming in and all sources of money going out

consumer: someone who buys and uses goods or services

credit union: an organization that is similar to a bank, except that it is owned by the people who deposit their money into it

economics: the study of money and how it is used

financial: relating to money

goal: a desired result

interest: money a bank pays a person for keeping his or her money in that bank

need: something a person must have to survive

opportunity cost: what you give up to pay for something else

tax: money collected by the government to pay for its activities and services

want: something a person would like but does not need

Learn More about Money

Books

Bochner, Arthur, Rose Bochner, and Adriane G. Berg. *New Totally Awesome Money Book For Kids (and Their Parents).* New York: Newmarket Press, 2007. Arthur first wrote this book when he was eleven. When he was twenty-four, he revised the book with his sister and mom, adding what they have all learned about finances.

Hall, Alvin D. *Show Me the Money.* New York: DK, 2008. Check out this book to learn more about the basic concepts of money, including the barter system and supply and demand.

Kemper, Bitsy. *Growing Your Money.* Minneapolis: Lerner Publications, 2015. This book explains several ways that you can use your money to make more money, including opening a savings account with interest.

Websites

Economics for Kids
http://www.socialstudiesforkids.com/subjects/economics.htm
From the history of money to how to set up your own lemonade stand, this friendly site shows how economics reaches into many parts of our lives.

It's My Life
http://pbskids.org/itsmylife/money/managing
Money professionals and real kids give details and information about tracking expenses, creating budgets, and more. They use real examples and give kids the chance to talk about their own experiences.

Kids.gov
http://kids.usa.gov/money
Visit this page to see how money is made, play games, and find out how to help your family save money.

055784244

Index

Photo Acknowledgments

The images in this book are used with the permission of: © Purestock/Thinkstock, p. 4; © Mega Pixel/Shutterstock Images, p. 5; © pio3/Shutterstock Images, p. 6; © Margot Petrowski/ Shutterstock Images, p. 7; © Pavel L Photo and Video/Shutterstock Images, p. 8; © Atlaspix/ Shutterstock Images, pp. 9, 15, 19, 25, 29, 33; © EPSTOCK/Shutterstock Images, p. 10; © Laura Westlund/Independent Picture Service, pp. 11, 27, 35; © Blend Images/Shutterstock Images, p. 12; © AVAVA/Shutterstock Images, p. 13; © Arina P Habich/Shutterstock Images, p. 14; © Feng Yu/ Shutterstock Images, p. 16; © karelnoppe/Shutterstock Images, p. 17; © Radius Images/Corbis, p. 18; © Carolyn Franks/Shutterstock Images, pp. 19, 33; © Fuse/Thinkstock, p. 20; © Anna Hoychuk/Shutterstock Images, p. 21; © bloomua/Shutterstock Images, p. 22; © travellight/ Shutterstock Images, p. 23; © ClassicStock/Corbis, p. 24; © Comstock Images/Stockbyte/ Thinkstock, p. 26; © JohnKwan/Shutterstock Images, p. 28; © Steve Hix/Somos Images/Corbis, p. 30; © Kunal Mehta/Shutterstock Images, p. 31; © OLJ Studio/Shutterstock Images, p. 32; © Robert Kneschke/Shutterstock Images, p. 34; © Darko Zeljkovic/Shutterstock Images, p. 36.

Front cover: © Stockbyte/Thinkstock (coins); © Laura Westlund/Independent Picture Service (illustration).

Main body text set in Adrianna Regular 14/20
Typeface provided by Chank